Lectin Free Slow Cooker Cookbook 2018

Top 70 Simple & Tasty Crock-Pot Slow Cooker Lectin-Free Recipes to Better Your Life, Have more Energy and Less Disease, Resist Inflammation and Be Longevity

Virginia C. Boin

INTRODUCTION

Chronic inflammation has been long considered to be one of the causes of many serious diseases that have been plaguing humanity ever since. Cancer, Alzheimer's, Diabetes, and Heart Diseases you name it!

Throughout the years, Scientists have been hard at work to find the core reason of Chronic Inflammation, and it seems like they may have finally cracked the code.

"Lectins" – illustrated in details by Steven Gundry in his amazing book titled "The Plant Paradox" are now being considered as being the real culprit for the increase inflammatory diseases.

Initially thought to be harmless, this protein is seemingly present a wide variety of foods that we previously considered to be "Healthy" and is slowly breaking down our body from the inside!

Afraid? Well, don't be! As the Lectins Free Diet is here to save the day.

Since the chapters and recipes in this book are dedicated towards beginners, I have written the first few chapters to fully explain the fundamental concepts of Lectins and Lectin Free diet while walking you through the basics of Slow Cooker as well.

Once you are done with the basics, the 70 amazing Lectin Free Slow Cooker recipes will inspire you to explore the Lectin Free Diet further and stay healthy in the long run!

Table of Contents

Chapter 11: Stocks And Sauces

Conclusion

Chapter 1: Basics Of Lectin Free Diet

What are Lectins?

In the simplest terms, Lectins are the proteins that are responsible for binding cell membranes together.

They have a sugar binding nature and are the "Glyco" section of Glycoconjugates present on cell membranes.

They help to assist other cells to interact with each other and joint together without the help of the immune mechanism. Lectins are considered to be a key factor when considering inter-cell bindings.

Why Are Lectins Bad?

While Lectin is found in almost all parts of the plants, the "Seeds" are the ones that humans tend to consume the most and are considered to be one of the original ways through which humans are exposed to Lectins.

According to various recent studies, it has been found that Lectins are incredibly toxic to the human body.

These harmful proteins tend to cause widespread inflammation all around the body, which leads to severe various side effects including, but not limited to unwanted weight gain, fogginess, and digestion issues and so on.

All these side-effects have given Lectins the notorious title of being "Anti-Nutrients" as they not only cause inflammation but also restrict the absorption of essential nutrients required by the body.

Looking At The Science Behind Lectins In Details

Lectins are generally carbohydrate-binding proteins that tend to attach to cell membranes. They tend to act as "Communicators" between other cells and allows them to interact with the environment and connect with each other.

Now it should be noted that there are different types of Lectins found in various living organisms. As mentioned above, the Lectins in plants are primarily located in their roots and seed with the lowest amount available in Leaves.

While there are thousands of different types of Lectins present, researchers took their time to break them down into 13 significant classifications with only two classes (namely agglutinins and prolamins) causing the most harm!

These two tend to cause a significant impact on how the gut and immune system of the body functions, causing a severe inflammatory response.

When your intestinal wall is permeated or damaged by these Lectins, proteins tend to leak out into the bloodstream.

At this time, the Lectin can bind to Glycoproteins that are found on the surface of most cells and antibodies, turning them into abnormal entities.

These abnormal cells travel to various parts of your body, which ultimately causes the body's natural response system to trigger the autoimmune response that leads to severe inflammation.

UNDERSTANDING THE CORE CONCEPTS OF LECTIN-FREE DIET

This particular form of diet was established by a former heart surgeon called Dr. Steven Gundry.

To summarize in brief, the Lectin Free diet is a form of elimination diet is very carefully and precisely designed to cut out any ingredients from an everyday food that may be considered to be packed with a high amount of Lectins.

Incidentally, due to our hectic schedule, we often eat various seemingly "Healthy" food that is packed with Lectins! We fail to understand the severe implications, and in the long run, they cause significant harm to the body.

And this is the point where we should discuss a little bit about inflammation.

WHAT ARE GLUTENS?

Before the discovery of Lectins, Glutens were perhaps one of the most controversial entities that often force people into debates of whether it was good or bad.

There is a powerful connection between Glutens and Lectins! But before establishing and explaining that, I do believe that it is essential for you to have an understanding of what "Glutens" actually are.

Strictly speaking, Glutens are a family of protein found in grains such as barley, wheat, rye, and spelled!

Perhaps the most common Gluten contain grain that we mostly consume is Wheat.

When flour is mixed up with water, Gluten is responsible for the texture that you get. This glue-like property helps the dough to be elastic and allows bread to rise when baked.

However, it seems that there is a large chunk of the population who are unable to tolerate gluten.

While most people can digest it just fine, others tend to suffer from various diseases such as wheat allergy, inflammation, irritable bowel syndrome, celiac diseases and so on.

THE ROLE OF GLUTEN IN THE DIET AND HOW IT AFFECTS HEALTH

Some people often consider that cutting down "Gluten" from their diet will naturally help them to stay healthy and fit!

Sound reasoning for this is the fact that Gluten is thought to be a type of Lectin, primarily belonging to the "Prolamin" class.

However, you should know by now that there are multiple classes of Lectins, and cutting down Glutens from your diet will only save you from one of the two harmful courses of Lectin.

You may still get Lectins from other different types of food if you are not careful!

WHAT IS INFLAMMATION?

And this brings us to our next issue with Lectins and Glutens, Inflammation.

It seems that amongst the many side effects of Lectins exposure, Inflammation stands at the top of the list! But what does inflammation mean?

Let me elaborate.

Inflammation is a vital aspect of our body's immune system and is an attempt to heal itself from any anomaly/defend itself from foreign organisms such as bacteria, virus and of course, repair damaged tissues.

Without natural inflammation, the wound's in our body would never heal and infections would eventually become deadly!

So far so good right?

However, this very effect can also cause extreme discomfort if "False" signals are sent to the body to initiate an unwanted inflammatory impact.

You should know that due to the nature of Inflammation, they have been divided into two categories, acute and chronic.

Acute inflammation is those that arise when you get a bruise, cut, sprained ankle, etc. These are the natural response of the body to heal yourself.

On the other hand, Chronic Inflammations are the "Bad" kind, and they are not useful to the body. Instead, they tend to occur due to certain diseases such as osteoarthritis and various auto-immune diseases such as lupus, allergies, inflammatory bowel disease, and rheumatoid arthritis and so on.

LINK BETWEEN LECTINS AND INFLAMMATION

So I have already established what Lectins and how damaging they are to the human body, I have explained what inflammation is!

Now, let make explain the correlation between these two.

Generally speaking, Lectins are thought to cause inflammation in the body that can occur in your bloodstream or just outside the digestive tract (Due to leakage of Lectins).

When this happens, our body starts to experience a wide range of symptoms depending on what we have eaten.

These range from bloating to severe vomiting or diarrhea.

Initially they stay at a tolerable level, however, if you keep exposing your body to more Lectins (as a result greater rate of inflammation), it is possible for these symptoms to grow into something severe and significantly damage the body.

Just as an eye opener, studies have shown that almost 20% of Rheumatoid arthritis are caused by consuming Lectin containing vegetables or ingredients!

THE INS AND OUTS OF LECTIN FREE DIET

That being said, you must be curious as to what you are allowed to eat and what you should avoid right?

Well, according to the creator of the diet, Dr. Gundry, you can go for the following foods when you are easing into the diet.

- Olive and Olive Oil: Olives are generally low in Lectin and are safe to consume on a Lectin free diet
- Avocado: Though it is a fruit, you can enjoy Avocados in Lectin free recipes
- Mushrooms: You can choose from a wide variety of mushrooms available in the market!
- Celery
- Asparagus
- Cruciferous Vegetables: Veggies such as Brussels, broccoli, cauliflower are veggies that are perfect to provide you with great nutrients while being low in Lectins
- Sweet Potatoes: Though potatoes are generally considered to be reached in Lectins, the sweet potatoes are amazing for Lectin Free diet. You will be able to enjoy the health benefits of potatoes while keeping your Lectins in check
- Casein A2 Milk: Always make sure to avoid Casein A2 Milk
- Pasture-raised meat: When considering meat, try to go for pasture-raised meat as they will help you meet up your daily protein need.

And on the opposite side of the coin, these are ingredients that you should try to avoid as much as possible to keep your Lectins down:

- Corn: This is a plant product that should be avoided at all cost as they are high on Lectins.
- Grains: Any grain should be avoided during this diet. However, if you have to go for grain, try to go for products that are made from White Flour instead of Wheat Flour as wheat flour contains more Lectins.
- Fruits: When considering fruit, always try to go for seasonal fruits
- Legumes such as beans, lentils, peas, and peanuts are to be avoided
- Squash
- All nightshade vegetables such as eggplant, peppers, potatoes tomatoes, etc. However, you should keep in mind that tomatoes and peppers can be used in moderate amount if you properly deseed them and peel them (peel in case of tomato). This helps to significantly lower the Lectin count when using these two ingredients in recipes.

HOW LECTIN NEGATIVELY AFFECTS HEALTH

Uncontrolled inflammation, which may result from excessive Lectin input leads to a wide variety of different harmful side effects.
Some of them include:

- **Type 1 Diabetes:** Type 1 Diabetes will cause the immune system to attack and destroy insulin-producing cells in your pancreas that will ultimately disrupt the regulation of sugar levels in your body.
- **Rheumatoid Arthritis:** RA causes the immune system to attack specific joints that results in considerable discomfort and pain.

- **Psoriatic Arthritis:** This causes the skin cell to multiply rapidly, which results in red and scaly patches called plaques on the skin.
- **Multiple Sclerosis:** MS tends to damage the protective coating that surrounds nerve cells (known as myelin sheath) and affects the transmission of a neural message between the brain and body. This often leads to weakness, balance issues, etc.
- **Inflammatory Bowel Syndromes:** This disease will irritate the intestinal lining.
- **Graves' Disease:** This disease attacks the thyroid gland in your neck and causes it to produce too much hormone, which results in a severe imbalance.
- **Cancer:** Cancerous tumors tend to secrete substances that attract cytokines and free-radicals that further cause inflammation and helps the tumors to survive. So, if you are already suffering from Anti-Inflammation, it will just make the condition of the Cancer much worse and help to grow and spread.
- **Alzheimer:** The brain does not have any pain receptors, but that doesn't mean that it won't be able to feel the effects of inflammation. Researchers have recently discovered that people a high level of Omega-6 fatty acids tend to have a higher chance of suffering from Alzheimer's disease, which just put is a disease and hampers your memory and makes you keep forgetting things from time to time.

LECTIN FREE SUBSTITUTION FOR THE PANTRY

While initially, you may start to feel that most of your favorite meals are packed with Lectins, and you won't be able to enjoy good food anymore!

I assure you that, it's not the case as there are some pretty good substitutes out there that will still allow you to enjoy your meals while staying Lectin free!

With the right ingredients by your side, you will easily be able to adapt to your new cooking and healthier lifestyle.

Some of the conventional substitutes are as follows:

- Replace wheat flour with almond flour
- Replace soy sauce with coconut aminos
- Replace regular mayonnaise with Duke's Mayonnaise
- Replace regular butter with ghee (clarified butter)
- Replace regular BBQ sauce with "NO Ketchup BBQ Sauce."
- Replace milk with almond milk or coconut milk
- Replace sugar with stevia
- Replace arrowroot powder instead of cornstarch

These tips should help you convert most of your standard recipes to Lectin Friendly ones.

ADVANTAGES OF LECTIN FREE DIET

While there are a lot of benefits that you can reap from a Lectin Free diet in the long term, some of the more crucial ones are as follows:

- You will lower the chances of suffering from chronic inflammation
- You will improve your heart condition
- It will protect you from cancer
- It will help you fend off depression
- It will help you to tackle various autoimmune diseases such as rheumatoid arthritis, diabetes and celiac diseases

And a lot of more!

FANTASTIC TIPS FOR LECTIN FREE JOURNEY

Asides from actually following the strict diet plan and cutting down on all sorts of Lectin ingredients, there are undoubtedly other steps that you can take in order to expand further the number of Lectins that you exposed to.

These extra steps rely on how you cook or prepare your foods. Let me break them down to you in details:

- **Pressure Cooking:** Pressure cooking has always been considered as one of the healthiest ways of preparing food as most of the nutrients are preserved correctly. However, the pressure cooker also does a great job of destroying the Lectins present in plants. So, if you are using ingredients such as beans, tomatoes, quinoa or even potatoes, pressure cooking them will ruin the Lectins and make them edible.
- **Choosing The Right Color:** Healthy food habits contribute to lowering down Lectins as well! However, there is a catch. People often recommend the "BROWN" of anything when considering healthy food. Brown rice, brown flour and so on. In case of Lectins though, it is advised that you do the exact opposite. The best step is to avoid grains altogether, but if you happen to go for grains, go for White Rice instead of brown and white bread instead of brown bread.
- **Peeling And Deseeding:** Majority of vegetables tend to have the highest concentration of Lectins in their skin and seeds. Thus it is always advised to peel and deseed fruits and vegetable thoroughly to reduce the amount of Lectins present.

Asides from those, you may also opt for

- Boiling
- Sprouting
- Fermenting

As well to lower down the Lectin count.

CHAPTER 2: EASING INTO THE DIET

With all that said and done, you must be wondering how you can start following the diet right?
Well, the best way to do this is to start your diet on a trial period and asses the future depending on the result.

START OFF WITH A TRIAL PERIOD

To start off, perhaps a good step would be to adjust a trial period of just 1 week. During this week, you will strictly adhere to the Lectin Free diet and make any and all necessary changes as required by the Lectin Free Diet.
You should keep in mind that during the first few days of your diet, you may experience some uneven symptoms, however, don't worry as these are temporary and will go away once your body habituates itself to the new diet.
However, if you feel that taking off all the Lectin Free food from your diet would be difficult, an alternative way to tackle this is to take off one Lectin Food off your regular dietary routine each week.
This will give you the chance to carefully measure the changes and help you understand which Lectin foods are the most sensitive and give you a broader idea of your Lectin intolerance.
If you are in a hurry, you can also opt for taking various Antibody tests that show certain types of Lectins, but these tests are not exhaustive and have the chance to give an unclear report.
Physicians and dieticians therefore always recommended to manually asses the impacts of taking off Lectin food one by one.
Now, the next step is to assess how you feel and what you should do. There are three things you can do from here:

WHAT TO DO IF YOU FEEL BETTER

If you think that cutting down your Lectin has improved your health, then the most appropriate thing to do is to consider extending the period of your test and think about following the diet in the long term.
The forward path will depend on how you followed the diet during your Test Period.
If you were daring enough to cut down all Lectin Free food at once, continue following that.
Else, if you were cutting down the Lectin packed food one by one, keep following that!
The goal here is to move on forward with the method that you most comfortable with.
Make sure to follow the cooking advice provided at the end of the chapter to decrease your Lectin count further.

Two important things to note:

- During this period, good advice is to track the Lectin free foods that are making you feel better. Try to incorporate those ingredients more into your recipes and create your diet regime surrounding those recipes.
- Also, try to measure how much better you are feeling reducing the Lectin free diet. You can track simple points such as any energy changes, sleep patterns, physical condition, etc. These will not only keep you motivated but will also help you assess your progress.

WHAT TO DO IF NOTHING HAS CHANGED

Once your trial period is over, if you see that there are no noticeable difference in your health, try to go back and assess what you may have done wrong.

Now naturally I don't encourage you to cut down all Lectin Food in one go (unless you are comfortable with it), the reason why you did not experience any difference might be the result of not cutting down enough Lectin from your diet.

In that case, you should go for another trial week and cut down more Lectin packed food compared to your previous week.

WHAT TO DO IF SITUATIONS HAVE GOTTEN WORSE

The worst case scenario is after the trial week; you might feel worse than you were feeling before!

This may happen for many different reasons, especially if you have any underlying health issues.

In this scenario, you should try to consult your doctor as soon as possible and perform any antibody test accordingly.

It will help you indicate if you have a specific intolerance to a small amount of Lectin classification.

CHAPTER 3: THE BASICS OF SLOW COOKER

With all the information regarding Lectin Diet out of the way, let me talk a little bit about your amazing Slow Cooker/CrockPot!
Since all the recipes in this book are crafted using a Slow Cooker, I believe that I should dedicate a chapter to it.
If you already have a Slow Cooker and have a good experience using it, then feel free to skip this chapter!
However, if the Slow Cooker is new to you, go ahead and have a look at this chapter as I will walk you through some of the basics of using the Slow Cooker.
Let's start with the most fundamental question first.

WHAT EXACTLY IS A SLOW COOKER?

The primary function of the Slow Cooker is to create mouthwatering and magnificent meals by cooking them over a prolonged period of low temperature.
Despite common believe though, Slow Cookers are incredibly versatile and easy to use, and they can cook a multitude of various dishes including but not limited to dips, roasts, stews, desserts, and even meats!
Going through the essential components of the Slow Cooker, you will notice that it contains an oval-shaped cooking pot made of high-quality glazed ceramic/porcelain.
This section houses the electrical circuitry of the Slow Cooker that controls everything.
Slow Cookers such as the Crock Pot comes with a glass lid as well that allows you to keep the Slow Cooker covered while letting you look through the lid and track the progress of your meal as well.
The condensed vapor produces inside the device creates a very low-effective pressure that seals the lid and helps it to stay firmly locked in place.
However, it should be noted that Slow Cookers are considerably safer to use when compared to other Pressure Cookers such, mainly because Slow Cookers tend to cook on a very low pressure as opposed to the high pressure utilized by pressure cookers.

SOME FANTASTIC ADVANTAGES OF SLOW COOKER

- Slow cooker generally helps to control the temptation of ordering takeout meal since making delicious meals using a cooker is extremely easy and requires minimum effort.
- Slow cookers are used all throughout the year! You can plop up a batch of hot soup in the winter and fabulous meals in the summer!
- Since the cooker uses a method of low temperature/ prolonged cooking, slow cookers help a lot to tenderize less-expensive meat cuts easily
- The slow cooking method dramatically helps to extract the full flavor of a meal! Not to mention the variety of different foods that you can cook, including but not limited to stews, meats, casseroles, soup and so on.!
- A slow cooker saves a lot of money since it uses much less energy than an oven!

WHAT "NOT" TO DO WHILE USING A SLOW COOKER

- Make sure never to add raw meat to your cooker
- Make sure never to use the wrong cut of meat. For a Slow Cooker, its best to stay away from expensive cuts
- Try to avoid opening the lid while the cooker is cooking!
- Make sure to avoid using too much wine or liquor
- If using dairy products, then don't use them early as they might start to curdle

GENERAL FEATURES OF THE SLOW COOKER

Asides from the advantages mentioned above, there are specific features of the Slow Cooker that you should know about that should make you love your device even more!

- **The Size:** The Slow Cooker's size allows an individual to create amazing dishes in bulk and feed a medium-sized family in one go!
- **The Programmable Cooking Times:** The Pre-Installed programs allows the cooking to act as an extremely versatile device that even enables amateur chefs to with no experience to cook perfect meals in a jiffy!
- **The "Warm" Setting:** The WARM setting of the Slow Cooker allows you to prepare meals ahead of time and keep them warm and fluffy up until the point you are ready to serve your meal!
- **The Digital Control Panel:** The digital control panel works to show you all the essential information that you need to know while cooking.
- **Easy To Use Insert:** Since the insert of the pot is easy to take out, it doesn't matter what you cook! You can take it out and wash it very quickly.

AMAZING SLOW COOKE TIPS TO FOLLOW!

The following Slow Cooker tips will help you to make amazing delicious dishes in no time!

- Make sure to buy the right sized Slow Cooker for you. Using a too large or small cooker will undercook or overcook your food
- Make sure to cut meat/vegetables in uniform equal sizes to ensure even cooking
- Try to trim as much fat as possible before placing meats in your Slow Cooker
- Make sure to avoid overcrowding your Slow Cooker as it will prevent the cooker from adequately cooking the meals
- Make sure to follow the times specified for the recipes to the tee! Otherwise, you may overcook your food.
- Try to avoid removing the lid during cooking. The escaped heat will add additional cooking time to your meal

Taking care of your Slow Cooker

Slow Cookers such as the CrockPot are already crafted to be extremely durable! However, you can make them last even longer by adequately following some easy steps.

- Make sure to unplug the Slow Cooker once your meal is cooked to avoid overcooking
- Pack any leftovers and let your Slow Cooker to cool before washing it. Make sure to remove the stoneware insert and fill it with warm soapy water and let it sit for a while to let the sticky food soften up
- Never use any abrasive scouring pads to clean your cooker. Use simple cloth, rubber or sponge to remove residues
- Never immerse the base of your cooker in liquid, keep it as dry as possible
- For cleaning the base, use a cloth dampened with warm and soapy water and wipe it gently
- While cooking, try to fill up the ceramic crock about halfway with liquid (as long as the recipe allows) for excellent results
- Like all ceramics, the stoneware insert is not designed to sustain dramatic heat changes, so let it cool completely before submerging it in water; otherwise, it may crack
- Don't use any metal utensils if your cooker, always go for Wooden, Silicone or Heatproof plastic utensils to avoid damaging the insert

Comparing Slow Cooking with other cooking methods

- If a meal takes typically 15-30 minutes, then it would take 1-2 hours on high settings or 4-6 hours on low settings in your crockpot.
- If a meal takes typically 30 minutes, then it would take 2-3 hours on high settings or 5-7 hours on low settings in your crockpot.
- If a meal takes typically 1 hour – 2 hours, then it would take 6-8 hours on high settings or 4-6 hours on low settings in your crockpot.
- If a meal takes typically 2 hours to 4 hours, then it would take 8-12 hours on high settings or 4-6 hours on low settings in your crockpot.

That being said, you are now ready to venture into the fantastic world of Slow Cooking! And with all of the that cleared up, you are now ready to dive into the fantastic world of Lectin Free Diet with your Slow Cooker!

VERY NUTTY FAUX "OATMEAL"

(Prepping time: 10 minutes \ Cooking time: 8 hours |For 6 servings)

Ingredients

- 1 tablespoon coconut oil
- 1 cup coconut milk
- 1 cup unsweetened shredded coconut
- ½ cup pecans, chopped
- ½ cup almonds, sliced
- 2 tablespoon stevia
- 1 avocado, diced
- 1 teaspoon ground cinnamon
- ¼ teaspoon ground nutmeg
- ½ cup blueberries, garnish

Directions

1. Grease the inner pot of your Slow Cooker with coconut oil
2. Place coconut milk, coconut, pecans, almonds, avocado, stevia, cinnamon and nutmeg to your Slow Cooker
3. Cover and cook on LOW for 8 hours
4. Stir the mix until you have your desired texture
5. Serve topped with blueberries
6. Enjoy!

Nutrition Values (Per Serving)

- Calories: 365
- Fat: 33g
- Carbohydrates: 10g
- Protein: 14g

(Prepping time: 10 minutes \ Cooking time: 3 hours | For 6 servings)

Ingredients

- 1 tablespoon extra-virgin olive oil
- 2 pounds ground pork
- 1 sweet onion, chopped
- ½ cup almond flour
- 2 teaspoon garlic, minced
- 2 teaspoon dried oregano
- 1 teaspoon dried thyme
- 1 teaspoon fennel seeds
- 1 teaspoon freshly ground black pepper
- ½ teaspoon salt
- 1 cup mashed banana or applesauce

Directions

1. Grease the insert of your Slow Cooker with olive oil
2. Take a large bowl and add pork, onion, banana/applesauce, almond flour, oregano, garlic, thyme, fennel seeds, pepper and salt
3. Mix well and pour the meat mix into the Slow Cooker
4. Shape it into loaf, leaving about ½ inch between the sides of the meat and inner pot wall
5. Cover and cook for 3 hours on LOW until the internal temperature reaches 150 degree Fahrenheit
6. Slice and serve
7. Enjoy!

Nutrition Values (Per Serving)

- Calories: 341
- Fat: 27g
- Carbohydrates: 1g
- Protein: 21g

(Prepping time: 15 minutes\ Cooking time: 6 hours |For 6 servings)

Ingredients

- 1 tablespoon extra-virgin olive oil
- 1 pound broccoli, cut into florets
- 1 pound cauliflower, cut into florets
- ¼ cup almond flour
- 2 cups coconut milk
- ½ teaspoon ground nutmeg
- Pinch of fresh ground black pepper
- 1 and ½ cups cashew cream

Directions

1. Grease the Slow Cooker inner pot with olive oil
2. Place broccoli and cauliflower to your Slow Cooker
3. Take a small bowl and stir in almond flour, coconut milk, pepper, 1 cup of cashew cream
4. Pour coconut milk mixture over vegetables and top casserole with remaining cashew cream
5. Cover and cook on LOW for 6 hours
6. Server and enjoy!

Nutrition Values (Per Serving)

- Calories: 377
- Fat: 32g
- Carbohydrates: 12g
- Protein: 16g

(Prepping time: 15 minutes\ Cooking time: 6 hours |For 4 servings)

Ingredients

- 2 tablespoons bacon fat
- 2 pounds kale, rinsed and chopped
- 2 bacon slices, cooked and chopped
- 2 teaspoons garlic, minced
- 2 cups vegetable broth
- Salt as needed
- Fresh ground black pepper

Directions

1. Grease the inner pot with bacon fat
2. Add kale, garlic, bacon, broth to insert and toss
3. Cover and cook on LOW for 6 hours
4. Season with salt and pepper
5. Serve and enjoy!

Nutrition Values (Per Serving)

- Calories: 147
- Fat: 10g
- Carbohydrates: 7g
- Protein: 7g

(Prepping time: 10 minutes\ Cooking time: 6 hours |For 4 servings)

Ingredients

- 3 tablespoons extra virgin olive oil
- 1 pound button mushrooms, wiped, cleaned and halved
- 2 teaspoons garlic, minced
- ¼ teaspoon salt
- 1/8 teaspoon fresh ground black pepper
- 2 tablespoons fresh parsley, chopped

Directions

1. Add olive oil, mushrooms, garlic, salt, pepper to your Slow Cooker
2. Cover and cook on LOW for 6 hours
3. Serve toss with parsley
4. Enjoy!

Nutrition Values (Per Serving)

- Calories: 58
- Fat: 5g
- Carbohydrates: 2g
- Protein: 2g

(Prepping time: 15 minutes\ Cooking time: 7-8 hours |For 4 servings)

Ingredients

- 1 tablespoon extra-virgin olive oil
- 1 small red cabbage, coarsely shredded
- ½ sweet onion, thinly sliced
- ¼ cup apple cider vinegar
- 3 tablespoon stevia
- 2 teaspoon garlic, minced
- ½ teaspoon ground nutmeg
- 1/8 teaspoon ground cloves
- 2 tablespoon ghee
- Salt as needed
- Fresh ground black pepper as needed
- ½ cup walnuts, chopped
- ½ cup cashew cream
- Peppercorns for garnish

Directions

1. Grease the Slow Cooker with olive oil
2. Add cabbage, onion, vinegar, stevia, nutmeg, garlic, cloves to insert
3. Stir well
4. Add ghee all over the cabbage mix
5. Cover and cook on LOW for 7-8 hours
6. Season with salt and pepper
7. Serve with topping of walnuts, cashew cream and peppercorns
8. Enjoy!

Nutrition Values (Per Serving)

- Calories: 152
- Fat: 12g
- Carbohydrates: 7g
- Protein: 4g

(Prepping time: 15 minutes\ Cooking time: 6 hours |For 4 servings)

Ingredients

- ½ cup extra virgin olive oil
- ¼ cup balsamic vinegar
- 1 tablespoon dried basil
- 1 teaspoon dried thyme
- ¼ teaspoon salt
- 2 cups cauliflower florets
- 1 yellow bell pepper, deseeded and cut into strips
- 1 cup button mushrooms, halved

Directions

1. Take a large bowl and add oil, basil, vinegar, thyme, salt and whisk
2. Add cauliflower, bell pepper, mushrooms and toss well to coat
3. Transfer the veggies to Slow Cooker
4. Cover and cook on LOW for 6 hours
5. Serve and enjoy!

Nutrition Values (Per Serving)

- Calories: 189
- Fat: 18g
- Carbohydrates: 5g
- Protein: 1g

(Prepping time: 10 minutes\ Cooking time:3-4 hours |For 4 servings)

Ingredients

- ½ cup coconut oil
- 2 teaspoons vanilla extract
- 1 teaspoon maple extract
- 1 cup pecans, chopped
- 1 cup sunflower seeds
- 1 cup unsweetened shredded coconut
- ½ cup hazelnuts
- ½ cup slivered almonds
- 2 tablespoon stevia
- ½ teaspoon cinnamon
- ¼ teaspoon ground nutmeg
- ¼ teaspoon salt

Directions

1. Grease the inner pot of your Slow Cooker with 1 tablespoon of coconut oil
2. Take a large bowl and add oil, vanilla and extract
3. Stir well and add pecans, coconut, sunflower seeds, hazelnuts, almonds, stevia, nutmeg, cinnamon and salt
4. Toss well
5. Transfer the mix to your Slow Cooker
6. Cover and cook on LOW for 3-4 hours
7. Transfer granola to baking sheet and cover with foil
8. Let it cool and serve as needed!

Nutrition Values (Per Serving)

- Calories: 236
- Fat: 23g
- Carbohydrates: 2g
- Protein: 6g

HEALTHY CHICKEN TACO DISH

(Prepping time: 10 minutes \ Cooking time: 6 hours |For 4 servings)

Ingredients

- 1 pound chicken breast
- 1 cup chicken broth
- 3 tablespoons taco seasoning

Directions

1. Take a bowl and mix taco seasoning and broth, keep it on the side
2. Grease your Slow Cooker with cooking spray and place the breast
3. Pour mix over meat and cover
4. Cook on MEDIUM for 6 hours
5. Let the chicken sit for a while
6. Open lid and shred chicken using fork
7. Serve with warm boiled sweet potatoes and your desired sauce

Nutrition Values (Per Serving)

- Calories: 409-
- Fat: 32g
- Carbohydrates: 13g
- Protein: 20g

(Prepping time: 15 minutes\ Cooking time: 7-8 hours |For 4 servings)

Ingredients

- 3 tablespoons coconut oil
- ¼ pound bacon, diced
- 2 pounds chicken, breast, thighs and drumsticks
- 2 cups quartered button mushrooms
- 1 sweet onion, diced
- 1 tablespoon garlic, minced
- ½ cup chicken broth
- 2 teaspoons thyme, chopped
- 1 cup coconut cream

Directions

1. Grease the insert of your Slow Cooker with 1 tablespoon of coconut oil
2. Take a large skillet and place it over medium high heat
3. Add 2 tablespoons of oil and let it heat up
4. Add bacon and cook until crispy, for about 5 minutes
5. Transfer bacon to plate and keep it on the side
6. Add chicken to skillet and brown for 5 minutes
7. Transfer chicken and bacon to Slow Cooker and add mushrooms, garlic, onion, broth and thyme
8. Cover and cook on LOW for 7-8 hours
9. Stir in coconut cream and serve
10. Enjoy!

Nutrition Values (Per Serving)

- Calories: 406
- Fat: 34g
- Carbohydrates: 5g
- Protein: 22g

(Prepping time: 10 minutes \ Cooking time: 2 hours 10 minutes |For 6 servings)

Ingredients

- 1 pack dry vegetable soup mix
- 2 pound duck roast
- 1 large onion
- 1 and ½ cups chicken broth
- 1 and ½ cups sweet potatoes, cubed

Directions

1. Grease the inner pot of your Slow Cooker
2. Add duck roast
3. Take a bowl and blend soup mix and chicken broth, keep it on the side
4. Cut onion in quarters and pull them apart
5. Transfer onion, sweet potatoes to the Slow Cooker and arrange them around the chicken
6. Pour soup mix over the top
7. Cover with lid and cook on HIGH for 2 hours
8. Let the meat sit for a while
9. Open lid and serve warm
10. Enjoy!

Nutrition Values (Per Serving)

- Calories: 525
- Fat: 51g
- Carbohydrates: 17g
- Protein: 2g

(Prepping time: 10 minutes | Cooking time: 8 hours |For 6 servings)

Ingredients

- 1 pound chicken breast, boneless and skinless
- 1 pound chick thigh, boneless and skinless
- 14 ounce artichoke hearts, drained
- 1 large onion, diced
- 2 medium carrots, diced
- 2 celery ribs, diced
- 3 garlic cloves, minced
- 1 bay leaf
- ½ teaspoon pepper
- 3 cups turnips, peeled and cubed
- 6 cups low sodium chicken broth
- ¼ cup freshly squeezed lemon juice
- ¼ cup parsley, chopped

Directions

1. Add the above mentioned ingredients to your cooker except lemon juice and parsley
2. Cook on LOW for 8 hours
3. Remove the chicken and shred it up
4. Return it back to the slow cooker
5. Season with some pepper and salt!
6. Stir in parsley and lemon juice and serve!

Nutrition Values (Per Serving)

- Calories: 400
- Fat: 10g
- Carbohydrates: 12g
- Protein: 3g

(Prepping time: 15 minutes \ Cooking time: 7-8 hours |For 4 servings)

Ingredients

- 3 tablespoons coconut oil
- ¼ pound bacon, diced
- 2 pounds chicken, breast, thighs and drumsticks
- 2 cups quartered button mushrooms
- 1 sweet onion, diced
- 1 tablespoon garlic, minced
- ½ cup chicken broth
- 2 teaspoons thyme, chopped
- 1 cup coconut cream

Directions

1. Grease Slow Cooker inner pot with 1 tablespoon oil
2. Rub remaining oil over chicken and season with salt and pepper
3. Stuff lemon quarters, garlic, thyme and bay leaves into cavity of chicken
4. Place onion quarters on the bottom of slow cooker
5. Place chicken on top
6. Cover and cook on LOW for 7-8 hours until the internal temperature reaches 165 degree Fahrenheit
7. Serve and enjoy!

Nutrition Values (Per Serving)

- Calories: 427
- Fat: 34g
- Carbohydrates: 2g
- Protein: 29g

(Prepping time: 10 minutes\ Cooking time: 7-8 hours |For 6 servings)

Ingredients

- 1 tablespoon extra-virgin olive oil
- 2 pounds boneless chicken thigh
- ½ cup chicken broth
- Juice and zest of 1 lemon
- 2 teaspoon garlic, minced
- 2 teaspoon paprika
- ½ teaspoon salt
- 1 cup cashew cream
- 1 tablespoon parsley, chopped

Directions

1. Lightly grease Slow Cooker with olive oil
2. Add chicken thigh to the Slow Cooker
3. Take a small bowl and add broth, lemon juice, garlic, zest, paprika and salt
4. Mix and pour broth over chicken
5. Cover and cook on LOW for 7-8 hours
6. Turn heat off and stir in cashew cream
7. Serve with a topping of parsley

Nutrition Values (Per Serving)

- Calories: 404
- Fat: 32g
- Carbohydrates: 4g
- Protein: 23g

(Prepping time: 10 minutes \ Cooking time: 4-6 hours |For 6 servings)

Ingredients

- 1 pound chicken breast, boneless and skinless
- ½ pound chicken thigh, boneless and skinless
- ½ small onion, diced
- 3 garlic cloves, minced
- 8 ounce pineapple, crushed
- 1/3 cup coconut aminos
- ½ teaspoon ginger, ground
- ¼ teaspoon red pepper flakes
- ½ teaspoon salt
- ¼ teaspoon pepper
- Swiss chard leaves/ lettuce leaves for wrap
- Avocado slices, shredded cabbage, carrot, sliced almonds, onion, fresh cilantro etc. for garnish

Directions

1. Add the onion, chicken and garlic to your Slow Cooker
2. Take a small sized bowl and add pineapple, lime juice, coconut aminos, red pepper flakes, salt and pepper
3. Stir well and cook on LOW for 4-6 hours
4. Remove the chicken and shred with fork
5. Return the shredded chicken to the Cooker and stir
6. Assemble your Swiss chard wraps by adding the chicken mix and topping them up with any of your garnish
7. Enjoy!

Nutrition Values (Per Serving)

- Calories: 170
- Fat: 5g
- Carbohydrates: 0g
- Protein: 10g

(Prepping time: 10 minutes\ Cooking time: 9 hours |For 4 servings)

Ingredients

- 3-4 pound whole chicken
- ¼ cup freshly squeezed lemon juice
- 1 teaspoon dried thyme
- 2-3 bay leaves
- 3-4 garlic cloves, peeled
- 1 teaspoon salt
- ¼ teaspoon black pepper

Directions

1. Remove the giblets from your chicken and rinse it under cool water
2. Add them to your slow cooker
3. Pour lemon juice over your whole chicken and sprinkle a bit of pepper, salt and thyme
4. Add the garlic cloves and bay leaves to the cooker and place them around the chicken
5. Cover the slow cooker and cook for about 9-10 hours under LOW setting
6. Once done, enjoy!

Nutrition Values (Per Serving)

- Calories: 490
- Fat: 16g
- Carbohydrates: 39g
- Protein: 45g

(Prepping time: 10 minutes \ Cooking time: 6 hours |For 4 servings)

Ingredients

- 1 tablespoon olive oil
- 1 cup leeks, chopped
- 2 garlic cloves, minced
- 1 and ½ tablespoon curry powder
- 1 cup almond milk
- ½ cup water
- 8 chicken thigh, skinless
- 1 and ½ cup celery, sliced diagonally
- 1 cup almonds, slivered and toasted

Directions

1. Take a heavy skillet and place it over medium heat
2. Add oil and allow the oil to heat up
3. Add leeks and Saute them
4. Transfer the leeks to your Slow Cooker
5. Add the rest of the ingredients to your Slow Cooker alongside slivered almonds
6. Cover with lid and cook on LOW for 6 hours
7. Scatter toasted almonds on top and enjoy!

Nutrition Values (Per Serving)

- Calories: 1222
- Fat: 98g
- Carbohydrates: 24g
- Protein: 67g

(Prepping time: 15 minutes \ Cooking time: 7-8 hours |For 6 servings)

Ingredients

- 3 tablespoons extra virgin olive oil
- 2 pounds boneless turkey legs
- Salt and pepper for seasoning
- 1 tablespoon dried thyme
- 2 teaspoon poultry seasoning
- ½ cup chicken broth
- 2 tablespoons fresh parsley, chopped, for garnish

Directions

1. Grease the Slow Cooker with 1 tablespoon olive oil
2. Take a large skillet and place it over medium-high heat
3. Add 2 tablespoons of olive oil
4. Season turkey with salt and pepper
5. Sprinkle thyme and poultry seasoning
6. Add turkey to skillet and brown for 7 minutes
7. Transfer turkey to Slow Cooker and add broth
8. Cover and cook on LOW for 7-8 hours
9. Serve with parsley
10. Enjoy!

Nutrition Values (Per Serving)

- Calories: 363
- Fat: 29g
- Carbohydrates: 1g
- Protein: 28g

COCONUT SHRIMP

(Prepping time: 5 minutes \ Cooking time: 2 hours |For 4 servings)

Ingredients

- 1 pound shrimp, with shells
- 3 and ¾ cups light coconut milk
- 1 and ¾ cups water
- ½ cup Thai Red curry sauce
- 2 and ½ teaspoons lemon garlic seasoning
- ¼ cup cilantro

Directions

1. Add coconut milk, red curry sauce, water, lemon garlic seasoning and cilantro to your Slow Cooker
2. Give it a nice stir
3. Cook on HIGH for 2 hours
4. Add shrimp and cook for another 15-30 minutes
5. Garnish with some cilantro and serve!

Nutrition Values (Per Serving)

- Calories: 576
- Fat: 22g
- Carbohydrates: 63g
- Protein: 32g

(Prepping time: 20 minutes\ Cooking time:2 hours |For 4 servings)

Ingredients

- A bunch of asparagus
- 4-6 Tilapia fillets
- 8-12 tablespoons lemon juice
- Pepper for seasoning
- Lemon juice for seasoning
- ½ tablespoon of clarified butter for each fillet

Directions

1. Cut single pieces of foil for the fillets
2. Divide the bundle of asparagus into even number depending on the number of your fillets
3. Lay the fillets on each of the piece of foil and sprinkle pepper and add a teaspoon of lemon juice
4. Add clarified butter and top with asparagus
5. Fold the foil over the fish and seal the ends
6. Repeat with all the fillets and transfer to cooker
7. Cook on HIGH for 2 hours
8. Enjoy!

Nutrition Values (Per Serving)

- Calories: 576
- Calories: 381
- Fat: 25g
- Carbohydrates: 4g
- Protein: 35g

(Prepping time: 10 minutes\ Cooking time: 2 hours 45 minutes |For 4 servings)

Ingredients

- 6 piece salmon fillets, skinless
- 1 large onion, chopped
- 6 garlic cloves, chopped
- 2 teaspoons ginger, grated
- 3 stalks celery, chopped
- 2 carrots, chopped
- 2 cans coconut milk
- ½ cup vegetable stock
- 1 and ½ teaspoon coriander
- 1 and ½ teaspoons cumin
- 1 teaspoon chili powder
- 1 cup red bell pepper paste
- 2 teaspoon smoked paprika
- 1 teaspoon turmeric
- ½ teaspoon pepper
- ½ teaspoon salt
- Cilantro, parsley, chili flakes, all chopped for garnish

Directions

1. Add 2 cans of coconut milk to the slow cooker
2. Add red bell pepper paste
3. Add vegetable stock, coriander, cumin, paprika, turmeric
4. Season with salt and pepper
5. Stir in the remaining ingredients
6. Place salmon pieces into the slow cooker and add onion, garlic, carrots, celery and ginger
7. Place lid and cook on LOW for 2 hours and 4 minutes
8. Garnish and serve!

Nutrition Values (Per Serving)

- Calories : 362
- Fat : 26g
- Carbohydrates : g
- Protein : 24g

(Prepping time: 5 minutes\ Cooking time:1 hour |For 4 servings)

Ingredients

- 2 tablespoon ghee
- 1 small onion, sliced
- 1 cup water
- ½ cup vegetable
- 4 salmon fillets
- 1 sprig fresh dill
- Sea salt as needed
- Black pepper as needed
- 1 quartered lemon, for garnish

Directions

1. Grease the slow cooker with ghee
2. Add onion slices to your pot and pour water
3. Add chicken broth
4. Cook on HIGH for 30 minutes (lid open)
5. Place fillets on top of the cooked onion and add lemon juice alongside fresh dill
6. Cover lid and cook on HIGH for 30 minutes more
7. Season with pepper and salt
8. Garnish with lemon and enjoy!

Nutrition Values (Per Serving)

- Calories: 576
- Calories: 381
- Fat: 25g
- Carbohydrates: 4g
- Protein: 35g

(Prepping time: 20 minutes\ Cooking time: 2 hours 30 minutes |For 4 servings)

Ingredients

- ¼ cup fish stock
- ½ cup white wine vinegar
- 2 tablespoons olive oil
- 2 teaspoon garlic clove, chopped
- 2 teaspoon parsley, minced
- 1 pound large sized raw shrimp

Directions

1. Add fish stock, lemon juice, white wine vinegar, olive oil, lemon juice, chopped garlic and fresh minced parsley
2. Add thawed shrimp (the ratio should be 1 pound of shrimp for ¼ cup of chicken broth)
3. Place lid and cook on LOW for 2 and a ½ hours
4. Serve and enjoy!

Nutrition Values (Per Serving)

- Calories : 293
- Fat : 24g
- Carbohydrates : 4g
- Protein : 16g

(Prepping time: 25 minutes \ Cooking time: 4 hours |For 5 servings)

Ingredients

- 2 tablespoons avocado oil
- 4 leeks, washed, trimmed and sliced
- 3 garlic cloves, minced
- 6 cups chicken broth
- 2 teaspoons dried thyme leaves
- 1 pound salmon, cut into bite sized portions
- 1 and ¾ cup of coconut milk
- Salt and pepper as needed

Directions

1. Add avocado oil to your Slow Cooker and set your cooker to HIGH
2. Allow it to heat and add chopped leeks, garlic and cook until tender
3. Pour chicken broth and thyme and simmer for 15 minutes
4. Season with salt and pepper
5. Add coconut milk and salmon to the pot
6. Place lid and cook on LOW for 4 hours until the fish is tender
7. Serve and enjoy!

Nutrition Values (Per Serving)

- Calories: 240
- Fat: 11g
- Carbohydrates: 14g
- Protein:14g

SUCCULENT POT ROAST

(Prepping time: 10 minutes\ Cooking time: 8 hours |For 6 servings)

Ingredients

- 2 pounds beef chuck roast, trimmed
- 1 pound russet potatoes, peeled and quartered
- 1 pound baby carrots
- 1 medium yellow onion, quartered
- 1 tablespoon steak seasoning
- ½ cup beef broth
- Salt
- Freshly ground black pepper

Directions

1. Cut roast into 4 equal pieces
2. Arrange beef, carrot, potatoes, onion in your Slow Cooker
3. Sprinkle beef and veggies with steak seasoning
4. Pour broth
5. Cover and cook on LOW for 8 hours
6. Transfer beef to cutting board and slice, transfer to serving dish
7. Serve with veggies and juice from slow cooker
8. Season with salt and pepper and enjoy!

Nutrition Values (Per Serving)

- Calories: 313
- Fat: 11g
- Carbohydrates: 19g
- Protein: 33g

CILANTRO AND LIME (SHREDDED) PORK

(Prepping time: 5 minutes\ Cooking time: 8 hours |For 6 servings)

Ingredients

- 2 and ½ pounds country style pork ribs, trimmed of fat
- ¼ cup fresh lime juice
- 1 tablespoon chili powder
- 1 tablespoon ground cumin
- 2 teaspoon salt
- ½ cup fresh cilantro, chopped

Directions

1. Add pork in slow cooker
2. Pour lime juice over pork and sprinkle chili powder, salt and cumin
3. Cover and cook on LOW for 8 hours
4. Transfer pork to cutting board and shred meat with two forks
5. Return pork to Slow Cooker and stir
6. Add chopped cilantro and serve
7. Enjoy!

Nutrition Values (Per Serving)

- Calories: 360
- Fat: 22g
- Carbohydrates: 2g
- Protein: 37g

(Prepping time: 15 minutes\ Cooking time: 10 hours |For 8 servings)

Ingredients

- 1 (5 pound) beef brisket, trimmed
- 2 teaspoons garlic powder
- 2 teaspoons chili powder
- 2 teaspoons salt
- ½ teaspoon freshly ground black pepper
- ½ cup ketchup
- 1/3 cup apple cider vinegar
- 2 tablespoons Worcestershire sauce (Go for Gluten free brand such as French's Worcestershire Sauce)
- 2 teaspoons Dijon mustard
- 2 tablespoon stevia
- 1 teaspoon garlic powder

Directions

1. Place brisket in your Slow Cooker
2. Take a small bowl and add garlic powder, salt, chili powder, pepper and rub the brisket with seasoning
3. Take a medium bowl and whisk ketchup, apple cider vinegar, Worcestershire sauce, Dijon mustard, stevia and garlic powder
4. Pour sauce over brisket
5. Cover and cook on LOW for 10 hours
6. Transfer brisket to cutting board
7. Cut in thin slices across grain
8. Return brisket to Slow Cooker and stir with the sauce
9. Enjoy!

Nutrition Values (Per Serving)

- Calories: 818
- Fat: 63g
- Carbohydrates: 10g
- Protein: 53g

(Prepping time: 10 minutes\ Cooking time: 8 hours |For 4 servings)

Ingredients

- 1 tablespoon extra-virgin olive oil
- 1 cup chicken broth
- 1 sweet onion, chopped
- ¼ cup Dijon mustard
- 1 teaspoon garlic, minced
- 1 teaspoon maple extract
- 4 boneless pork chops (4 ounce each)
- 1 cup cashew cream
- 1 teaspoon fresh thyme , chopped

Directions

1. Grease the insert of Slow Cooker with olive oil
2. Add broth, onion, garlic, Dijon mustard, maple extract to the Insert
3. Stir well
4. Add pork chops
5. Cover and cook on LOW for 8 hours
6. Stir in cashew cream
7. Serve with topping of thyme
8. Serve and enjoy!

Nutrition Values (Per Serving)

- Calories: 490
- Fat: 42g
- Carbohydrates: 5g
- Protein: 22g

(Prepping time: 10 minutes \ Cooking time: 9 hours |For 6 servings)

Ingredients

- 1 (2 pound) pork shoulder, trimmed
- ½ cup chicken broth
- 1 tablespoon coconut aminos
- 1 tablespoon liquid smoke
- 1 garlic clove, minced

Directions

1. Cut pork roast into four even pieces and transfer to your Slow Cooker
2. Pour broth, aminos, liquid smoke and garlic over pork
3. Cover and cook on LOW for 9 hours
4. Transfer pork to carving board and shred it
5. Serve and enjoy!

Nutrition Values (Per Serving)

- Calories: 392
- Fat: 31g
- Carbohydrates: 0g
- Protein: 26g

PORK AND BROCCOLI DELIGHT

(Prepping time: 10 minutes \ Cooking time: 8 hours | For 6 servings)

Ingredients

- 1 cup beef broth
- ½ cup coconut aminos
- ¼ cup oyster sauce
- 1 teaspoon toasted sesame oil
- 2 tablespoon stevia
- 1 teaspoon garlic powder
- 2 pounds pork stew meat
- ¼ cup arrowroot starch
- ¼ cup water
- 1 pack (16 ounce) frozen broccoli

Directions

1. Add beef broth, oyster sauce, coconut aminos, sesame oil, stevia, garlic powder to your Slow Cooker
2. Whisk well
3. Add pork and stir to coat with the sauce
4. Cover and cook on LOW for 8 hours
5. Remove lid and set Slow Cooker to HIGH
6. Make a slurry by whisking arrowroot and water in a small bowl, add the slurry to the liquid and stir
7. Add frozen broccoli in colander and run hot water through it until warmed
8. Shake excess liquid
9. Stir broccoli into slow cooker
10. Let the sauce thicken for 10 minutes
11. Serve and enjoy!

Nutrition Values (Per Serving)

- Calories: 319
- Fat: 12g
- Carbohydrates: 17g
- Protein: 34g

(Prepping time: 10 minutes \ Cooking time: 8 hours |For 6 servings)

Ingredients

- 1 beef short rib
- 2 small red onions, chopped
- 2 garlic cloves, minced
- 2 star anise
- 1 teaspoon ginger, ground

Directions

1. Process and prepare the ingredients accordingly
2. Chop the onions and crush the garlic
3. Add beef to your Slow Cooker
4. Add garlic, onion, ginger, star anise on top of the meat
5. Add water of about 1 inch depth
6. Place the lid and cook on LOW for 8 hours
7. Season and serve with veggies!

Nutrition Values (Per Serving)

- Calories: 105
- Fat: 7g
- Carbohydrates: 0g
- Protein: 11g

48

(Prepping time: 10 minutes\ Cooking time: 8-10 hours |For 6 servings)

Ingredients

- 3 pound pork shoulder (ethically raised)
- 1 cup bone broth
- 6 sprigs fresh rosemary
- 4 sprigs basil leaves
- 1 tablespoon chives, chopped
- ½ teaspoon sea salt
- ¼ teaspoon ground black pepper
- 3 organic pink lady apples, chopped

Directions

1. Turn your slow cooker to LOW and all of the listed ingredients
2. Cook on LOW for about 8-10 hours
3. Slice the roast into smaller pieces if preferred and serve!

Nutrition Values (Per Serving)

- Calories: 248
- Fat: 8g
- Carbohydrates: 0.7g
- Protein: 39g

(Prepping time: 10 minutes\ Cooking time: 9 hours |For 6 servings)

Ingredients

- ½ cup chicken broth
- 2 medium yellow onion, halved and thinly sliced
- 1 and ½ pounds white mushrooms, sliced
- 1 teaspoon dried thyme
- 6 (6 -8 ounce) beef blade steaks
- ½ teaspoon salt
- ¼ teaspoon freshly ground black pepper
- 2 tablespoons fresh parsley, minced
- 1/3 cup coconut cream

Directions

1. Add broth, onions,mushrooms, thyme in your Slow Cooker
2. Place beef on top veggies and season with salt and pepper
3. Cover and cook on LOW for 9 hours
4. Transfer steak to platter and tent with aluminum foil
5. Let the liquid settle for 5 minutes in the pot, skim off any extra fat from the surface using a large spoon
6. Stir in cream and parsley into the cooker
7. Season with salt and pepper
8. Serve steaks with the sauce
9. Serve and enjoy!

Nutrition Values (Per Serving)

- Calories: 466
- Fat: 23g
- Carbohydrates: 9g
- Protein: 54g

Ultimate Buffalo Pork Lettuce Wraps

(Prepping time: 5 minutes\ Cooking time: 8 hours |For 6 servings)

Ingredients

- 1 whole (2 pound) picnic pork roast, trimmed
- 1 small yellow onion, quartered
- 1 cup chicken broth
- ½ cup buffalo sauce
- 6 large romaine leaves

Directions

1. Add pork roast in Slow Cooker
2. Nestle onion quarters around pork
3. Pour broth over pork
4. Cover and cook on LOW for 8 hours
5. Transfer pork to cutting board and shred using two forks
6. Discard onion and liquid from the cooker
7. Transfer shredded meat back to the cooker
8. Pour buffalo sauce and stir
9. Place a heaping portion of pork mix on each romaine leaf and roll
10. Serve and enjoy!

Nutrition Values (Per Serving)

- Calories: 400
- Fat: 31g
- Carbohydrates: 2g
- Protein: 26g

(Prepping time: 5 minutes\ Cooking time: 7 hours |For 6 servings)

Ingredients

- 2 pounds extra lean ground beef
- 1/3 cup coconut aminos
- 2 tablespoons toasted sesame oil
- 2 teaspoons fresh ginger, minced
- 2 tablespoon stevia
- 2 teaspoons garlic powder
- ½ teaspoon red pepper flakes
- Chopped scallions, garnish

Directions

1. Add beef in Slow Cooker and break it using wooden spoon
2. Take a small bowl and whisk in coconut aminos, sesame oil, ginger, stevia, garlic powder, red pepper flakes and stir well
3. Stir the mixture into beef and coat it well
4. Cover and cook on LOW for 7 hours
5. Stir the beef mix again and break it up into smaller chunks
6. Garnish with scallions
7. Enjoy!

Nutrition Values (Per Serving)

- Calories: 372
- Fat: 18g
- Carbohydrates: 15g
- Protein: 33g

Ginger Pork And Sweet Potato Chowder

(Prepping time: 20 minutes\ Cooking time: 6 hours 15 minutes to 8 hours 20 minutes |For 4 servings)

Ingredients

- 1 /3 pound pork loin, cut into 1 and ½ inch cubes
- 2 leeks, chopped
- 4 large sweet potatoes, peeled and cubed
- 4 garlic cloves, minced
- 3 tablespoon grated fresh ginger root
- 1 teaspoon ground ginger
- 8 cups roasted vegetable broth
- 2/3 cup almond milk
- 2 tablespoons arrowroot

Directions

1. Add pork, sweet potatoes, leeks, garlic, ginger root, ground ginger, vegetable broth to your Slow Cooker
2. Cook on LOW for 6-8 hours until the potatoes are tender
3. Take a small bowl and whisk in coconut milk and arrowroot, mix well
4. Stir the mixture into the slow cooker
5. Cover and cook on LOW for 15-20 minutes more until the chowder is thick
6. Serve and enjoy!

Nutrition Values (Per Serving)

- Calories: 382
- Fat: 8g
- Carbohydrates: 33g
- Protein: 42g

(Prepping time: 10 minutes\ Cooking time: 5 hours |For 4 servings)

Ingredients

- 3 garlic cloves, minced
- ¼ teaspoon salt
- ¼ teaspoon ground black pepper
- 4 (4 ounce) boneless top round lamb steaks, trimmed
- ½ cup chicken broth
- 1 tablespoon fresh basil, chopped
- 1 tablespoon mint, chopped
- ¼ cup bell pepper, sliced and chopped, deseeded

Directions

1. Take a small bowl and stir minced garlic, salt, pepper
2. Rub lamb steak with the garlic mix and transfer to Slow Cooker
3. Pour broth
4. Cover and cook on LOW for 5 hours
5. Transfer lamb steak to serving platter
6. Season with more salt and pepper
7. Garnish with sprinkle of basil, mint and bell peppers
8. Enjoy!

Nutrition Values (Per Serving)

- Calories: 301
- Fat: 24g
- Carbohydrates: 3g
- Protein: 19g

Juicy Vegetable Beef Roast

(Prepping time: 10 minutes\ Cooking time: 9 hours |For 6 servings)

Ingredients

- 3-4 pound beef roast
- ½ teaspoon salt
- Olive oil
- ¼ teaspoon pepper
- 1 and ½ pound red potatoes
- 1 small white onion
- 1 and ½ pound carrots, peeled
- 1 garlic clove, minced
- 1 teaspoon dried thyme
- 1 teaspoon dried oregano
- 1/3 cup balsamic vinegar

Directions

1. Sprinkle your roast and season it with pepper and salt
2. Place a pan over medium high heat and add oil, allow the oil to heat up
3. Once the oil is hot, transfer the meat to the pan and brown on all sides
4. Transfer the cooked roast to your slow cooker
5. Add onions and potatoes around the roast
6. Sprinkle oregano, thyme and garlic
7. Drizzle your balsamic and vinegar
8. Add carrots on top of your roast
9. Cover it up and cook on LOW for about 8 hours
10. Shred the meat and serve with potatoes, onion and carrots
11. Drizzle the cooking juices over
12. Have fun!

Nutrition Values (Per Serving)

- Calories: 300
- Fat: 8g
- Carbohydrates: 26g
- Protein: 24g

(Prepping time: 10 minutes\ Cooking time: 8 hours |For 6 servings)

Ingredients

- ½ a cabbage, roughly sliced
- 1 whole onion, diced
- 3 garlic cloves, finely chopped
- 1 and ½ pound ground beef
- 1 and ½ cups red bell pepper, deseeded and sliced
- 2 cups cauliflower rice
- 4 tablespoons ghee
- 1 heaping tablespoon of Italian seasoning
- ½ teaspoon of crushed red pepper
- Salt as needed
- ½ cup fresh parsley, finely chopped

Directions

1. Add the listed ingredients to your Slow Cooker (except parsley) and give it a nice stir
2. Place lid and cook on LOW for 7-8 hours until the beef is coked
3. Stir in parsley and serve
4. Enjoy!

Nutrition Values (Per Serving)

- Calories: 320
- Fat: 18g
- Carbohydrates: 0g
- Protein: 17g

Chapter 8: Vegan And Vegetarian Recipes

Super Baked Apple Dish

(Prepping time: 10 minutes \ Cooking time: 4 hours 15 minutes | For 4 servings)

Ingredients

- 5 medium apples
- ½ teaspoon nutmeg powder
- ½ teaspoon cinnamon powder
- 2 drops stevia
- 1 cup walnuts
- Ghee for greasing

Directions

1. Peel the apples about fourth of the way down and remove cores and seeds
2. Take a bowl and add the remaining mixture and mix them well
3. Fill the peeled apples with the prepared mixture
4. Grease your Slow Cooker with ghee
5. Grease the outer part of your apples with ghee as well
6. Transfer apples to your Slow Cooker and put lid
7. Cook on LOW for 4 hours
8. Remove lid immediately and remove apples
9. Let them reach room temperature and serve
10. Enjoy!

Nutrition Values (Per Serving)

- Calories: 152
- Fat: 2g
- Carbohydrates: 35g
- Protein: 1g

(Prepping time: 10 minutes\ Cooking time: 8 hours |For 4 servings)

Ingredients

- 4 Yukon Gold potatoes, chopped
- 2 russet potatoes, chopped
- 1 large parsnip, peeled and chopped
- 3 large carrots, peeled and chopped
- 2 onions, chopped
- 2 garlic cloves, minced
- 2 tablespoons olive oil
- ¼ cup roasted vegetable broth
- ½ teaspoon salt
- 1 teaspoon dried thyme leaves

Directions

1. Add the listed ingredients to your Slow Cooker
2. Stir well
3. Cover and cook on LOW for 7-8 hours
4. Stir hash and enjoy

Nutrition Values (Per Serving)

- Calories: 150
- Fat: 0g
- Carbohydrates: 28g
- Protein: 3g

(Prepping time: 20 minutes \ Cooking time: 9 hour |For 8 servings)

Ingredients

- 6 Yukon Gold Potatoes, thinly sliced
- 3 sweet potatoes, thinly sliced and peeled
- 2 onions, thinly sliced
- 4 garlic cloves, minced
- 3 tablespoons almond flour
- 4 cups almond milk
- 1 and1/2 cups roasted veggie broth
- 3 tablespoons ghee
- 1 teaspoon dried thyme leaves
- 1 and ½ cup cashew cream

Directions

1. Grease your slow cooker with olive oil
2. Layer potatoes, onion and garlic
3. Take a large bowl and add flour, ½ cup milk and stir well
4. Stir in broth, ghee, thyme leaves
5. Pour milk mix over potatoes
6. Top with cashew cream
7. Cover and cook for 7-9 hours
8. Enjoy!

Nutrition Values (Per Serving)

- Calories: 415
- Fat: 22g
- Carbohydrates: 42g
- Protein: 17g

(Prepping time: 20 minutes\ Cooking time: 8-10 hour |For 3 servings)

Ingredients

- 10 large yellow onions, peeled and sliced
- 20 garlic cloves, peeled
- ¼ cup olive oil
- ¼ teaspoon salt
- 2 tablespoons balsamic vinegar
- 1 teaspoon dried thyme leaves

Directions

1. Add the listed ingredients to your Slow Cooker
2. Stir well
3. Cover and cook on LOW for 8-10 hours
4. Serve and enjoy!

Nutrition Values (Per Serving)

- Calories: 109
- Fat: 4g
- Carbohydrates: 16g
- Protein: 2g

(Prepping time: 10 minutes \ Cooking time: 3-4 hours | For 8 servings)

Ingredients

- 2 and ½ pound sweet potatoes, peeled
- 1 cup water
- 1 tablespoon fresh ginger, grated
- ½ teaspoon ginger, minced
- ½ tablespoon ghee

Directions

1. Peel the potatoes and quarter them
2. Add them to the slow cooker
3. Add water, fresh ginger and ginger
4. Stir well
5. Cook on HIGH for 3-4 hours until the potatoes are tender
6. Add ghee and mash them
7. Serve immediately and enjoy!

Nutrition Values (Per Serving)

- Calories: 100
- Fat: 0.5g
- Carbohydrates: 23g
- Protein: 2g

(Prepping time: 15 minutes \ Cooking time: 6-8 hour |For 6 servings)

Ingredients

- 2 cups dried apricot
- 2 cups prunes
- 2 cups pears
- 2 cups dried apples
- 1 cup dried cranberries
- 2 tablespoons stevia
- 6 cups water
- 1 teaspoon dried thyme leaves
- 1 teaspoon dried basil leaves

Directions

1. Add the listed ingredients to your Slow Cooker
2. Cover and cook on LOW for 6-8 hours
3. Serve and enjoy!

Nutrition Values (Per Serving)

- Calories: 242
- Fat: 0g
- Carbohydrates: 61g
- Protein: 2g

BEET AND ONION DELIGHT

(Prepping time: 20 minutes \ Cooking time: 5-7 hour |For 6 servings)

Ingredients

- 10 medium beets, peeled and diced
- 3 red onions, chopped
- 4 garlic cloves, minced
- 2 tablespoons stevia
- 1/3 cup lemon juice
- 1 cup water
- 2 tablespoons melted coconut oil
- 3 tablespoons arrowroot
- ½ teaspoon salt

Directions

1. Add beets, onion and garlic to your Slow Cooker
2. Take a medium bowl and add stevia, lemon juice, coconut oil, water, arrowroot, salt and stir until combined
3. Pour mixture over beets
4. Cover and cook for 5-7 hours until the beets are tender
5. Enjoy!

Nutrition Values (Per Serving)

- Calories: 140
- Fat: 4g
- Carbohydrates: 27g
- Protein: 2g

(Prepping time: 20 minutes\ Cooking time: 4 hours |For 3 servings)

Ingredients

- 2 bunch Swiss Chard, washed and cut into large pieces
- 2 bunch collard greens, washed and cut into large pieces
- 2 bunch kale, washed and cut into large piece
- 3 onions, chopped
- 1 and ½ cups roasted vegetable broth
- 1 tablespoon stevia
- 2 tablespoons lemon juice
- 1 teaspoon dried marjoram
- 1 teaspoon dried basil
- ¼ teaspoon salt

Directions

1. Add Swiss Chard, Collard Green Kale and onions to your Slow Cooker
2. Stir well
3. Take a medium bowl and add broth, nectar, lemon juice, basil, marjoram, salt and basil
4. Mix well and add to the Slow Cooker
5. Close and cook on LOW for 3-4 hours
6. Enjoy!

Nutrition Values (Per Serving)

- Calories: 80
- Fat: 0g
- Carbohydrates: 19g
- Protein: 3g

FRUIT AND LEMON COMPOTE

(Prepping time: 10 minutes \ Cooking time: 1 hours 45 |For 4 servings)

Ingredients

- 3 green tea bags
- 3 and ¼ cup boiling water
- 2 tablespoons stevia
- 2 teaspoon freshly grated lemon zest
- 3 cups mixed dried fruits such as apples, apricot, peat etc.

Directions

1. Seep the tea bags under boiling water for 5 minutes
2. Remove the tea bag and stir in sugar
3. Add zest
4. Cut the large fruits into quarters and half the quarters
5. Add them to your Slow Cooker
6. Pour tea
7. Submerge and place the lid, cook on HIGH for ½ to 2 hours
8. Once the fruit is syrupy, enjoy!

Nutrition Values (Per Serving)

- Calories : 236
- Fat : 43g
- Carbohydrates : 26g
- Protein : 2g

(Prepping time: 20 minutes\ Cooking time: 6 hours |For 4 servings)

Ingredients

- 1 tablespoon extra-virgin olive oil
- 4 cups cauliflower florets
- 1 carrot, diced
- 1 red bell pepper, diced and deseeded
- 2 cups coconut milk
- ½ sweet onion, chopped
- 1 tablespoon fresh ginger, grated
- 2 teaspoon garlic, minced
- 2 teaspoon ground cumin
- 1 teaspoon ground coriander
- ½ teaspoon turmeric
- ¼ teaspoon cardamom
- ¼ teaspoon cayenne pepper
- 2 tablespoon cilantro, chopped

Directions

1. Grease the inner pot of your Slow Cooker with olive oil
2. Add cauliflower, carrot and bell pepper to your Slow Cooker
3. Take a small bowl and whisk coconut milk, chipotle pepper, onion, ginger, garlic, cumin, coriander turmeric, cayenne pepper and cardamom
4. Pour the mixture over Slow Cooker
5. Stir
6. Cover and cook on LOW for 6 hours
7. Serve with a garnish of cilantro
8. Enjoy!

Nutrition Values (Per Serving)

- Calories: 299
- Fat: 23g
- Carbohydrates: 9g
- Protein: *g

(Prepping time: 20 minutes\ Cooking time: 4 hours |For 4 servings)

Ingredients

- 2 heads, cauliflower, rinsed and cut into florets
- 2 onions, chopped
- ½ cup orange juice
- 1 teaspoon grated orange zest
- 1 teaspoon dried thyme leaves
- ½ teaspoon dried basil leaves
- ½ teaspoon salt

Directions

1. Add cauliflower, onion to your Slow Cooker
2. Mix and top with orange juice, orange zest ad drizzle thyme, basil and salt
3. Cover and cook on LOW for 4 hours
4. Pierce with fork and enjoy!

Nutrition Values (Per Serving)

- Calories: 75
- Fat: 0g
- Carbohydrates: 16g
- Protein: 5g

(Prepping time: 20 minutes\ Cooking time: 5 hours |For 3 servings)

Ingredients

- 4 bunch kale, washed, stemmed and cut into large pieces
- 2 onions, choppe
- 8 garlic cloves, minced
- 2 jalapeno peppers, minced
- 4 large red bell peppers, deseeded, sliced
- 1 tablespoon chili powder
- ½ teaspoon salt
- 1/8 teaspoon freshly ground black pepper

Directions

1. Add kale, onions, jalapeno peppers, garlic, bell pepper to your Slow Cooker
2. Sprinkle chili powder, salt and pepper and stir
3. Cover with lid and cook on LOW for 4-5 hours until the kale is tender
4. Serve and enjoy!

Nutrition Values (Per Serving)

- Calories: 52
- Fat: 1g
- Carbohydrates: 11g
- Protein: 3g

(Prepping time: 20 minutes\ Cooking time: 6-8 hours |For 4 servings)

Ingredients

- 4 large carrots, peeled and cut into chunks
- 2 onions, peeled and sliced
- 6 garlic cloves, peeled and sliced
- 2 parsnips, peeled and sliced
- 2 jalapeno peppers, minced
- ½ cup roasted vegetable broth
- ½ cup of canned coconut milk
- 3 tablespoons lime juice
- 2 tablespoons grated fresh ginger root
- 2 teaspoons curry powder

Directions

1. Add carrots, onions, parsnips, garlic, jalapeno peppers to your Slow Cooker
2. Take a small bowl and add broth, coconut milk, ginger root, lime juice, curry powder and blend well
3. Pour mix into Slow Cooker
4. Cover and cook on LOW for 6-8 hours
5. Serve and enjoy!

Nutrition Values (Per Serving)

- Calories: 69
- Fat: 3g
- Carbohydrates: 13g
- Protein: 1g

Blissful Turkey Spinach Soup

(Prepping time: 10 minutes | Cooking time: 8 hours | For 4 servings)

Ingredients

- 4 cups baby spinach
- 1 tablespoon oregano
- 1 tablespoon ginger, minced
- 1 cup turkey meat, boiled and cubed
- Salt
- Red chili flakes

Directions

1. Add all the listed ingredients to your Slow Cooker except meat
2. Add enough water to cover them
3. Close lid and cook on LOW for 7 hours
4. Let the soup sit for a while
5. Open lid and use immersion blender to smoothen the soup
6. Add cooked turkey cubes and close lid
7. Cook on LOW for 1 hour more
8. Stir and serve
9. Enjoy!

Nutrition Values (Per Serving)

- Calories: 215
- Fat: 7g
- Carbohydrates: 19g
- Protein: 18g

BACON AND SPINACH SOUP

(Prepping time: 10 minutes \ Cooking time: 3 hours 15 minutes |For 4 servings)

Ingredients

- 3 cups baby spinach
- ½ cup sweet potato
- ½ cup broccoli florets
- 2 tablespoons ginger, minced
- 2 tablespoons garlic cloves, minced
- Salt as needed
- Red chili flakes as needed
- 3 bacon slices
- 3 cups vegetable broth

Directions

1. Cook bacon slices in your Slow Cooker until they are crispy, keep them on the side
2. Add the remaining ingredients in the leftover bacon grease in your Slow Cooker
3. Close lid and cook on LOW for 3 hours
4. Let the soup sit for a while
5. Crumbled the crisped bacon slices and add them to the soup
6. Stir well and cook for 5 minutes more (lid off)
7. Season accordingly and enjoy!

Nutrition Values (Per Serving)

- Calories: 339
- Fat: 18g
- Carbohydrates: 32g
- Protein: 13g

(Prepping time: 10 minutes\ Cooking time: 6 hours 5 minutes |For 4 servings)

Ingredients

- 1 cup onion, chopped
- 1 cup Sautéed sausages, cubed
- 2 tablespoon ginger, minced
- Salt as needed
- Red chili flakes as needed
- 3 cups mushroom stock

Directions

1. Add the listed ingredients to your Slow Cooker
2. Close lid and cook on LOW for 6 hours
3. Let the soup sit for a while
4. Open lid and stir thoroughly
5. Let it cook for 5 minutes more without lid
6. Serve with your desired seasoning
7. Enjoy!

Nutrition Values (Per Serving)

- Calories: 269
- Fat: 9g
- Carbohydrates: 39g
- Protein: 10g

(Prepping time: 10 minutes\ Cooking time: 3 hours 5 minutes |For 4 servings)

Ingredients

- 2 and ½ cups Swiss chard, chopped
- 2 tablespoons ginger, minced
- 1 cup onion, chopped
- 1 teaspoon oregano
- Salt as needed
- Red chili flakes as needed

Directions

1. Add the listed ingredients to your Slow Cooker
2. Add enough water to cover the ingredients
3. Close lid and cook on MEDIUM for 3 hours
4. Let it sit for a while
5. Open lid and use immersion blender to blend the soup into a creamy texture
6. Stir and enjoy with more seasoning if needed

Nutrition Values (Per Serving)

- Calories: 284
- Fat: 19g
- Carbohydrates: 13g
- Protein: 15g

(Prepping time: 10 minutes \ Cooking time: 3 hours 5 minutes |For 4 servings)

Ingredients

- 1 tablespoon ginger, minced
- 1 teaspoon lemon juice
- 3 cups cauliflower florets
- ½ teaspoon hot sauce
- Salt as needed
- Red chili flakes as needed

Directions

1. Add the listed ingredients to your Slow Cooker
2. Add 2 cups of water
3. Stir and put lid
4. Cook on MEDIUM for 3 hours
5. Let it sit for a while
6. Remove lid and blend using an immersion blender to make the soup creamy and smooth
7. Stir the soup well and seasoning according to your taste
8. Serve and enjoy!

Nutrition Values (Per Serving)

- Calories: 412
- Fat: 18g
- Carbohydrates: 43g
- Protein: 22g

FEISTY CRAB SOUP

(Prepping time: 10 minutes\ Cooking time: 3 hours 5 minutes |For 4 servings)

Ingredients

- 1 cup crab meat, cubed
- 1 tablespoon garlic, minced
- Salt as needed
- Red chili flakes as needed
- 3 cups vegetable broth
- 1 teaspoon salt

Directions

1. Coat the crab cubes in lime juice and let them sit for a while
2. Add the all ingredients (including marinated crab meat) to your Slow Cooker and put lid
3. Cook on MEDIUM for 3 hours
4. Let it sit for a while
5. Remove lid and simmer the soup for 5 minutes more on LOW
6. Stir and check seasoning
7. Enjoy!

Nutrition Values (Per Serving)

- Calories: 201
- Fat: 11g
- Carbohydrates: 12g
- Protein: 13g

(Prepping time: 10 minutes\ Cooking time: 4 hours 20 minutes |For 4 servings)

Ingredients

- 3 pounds apples
- Pinch of ground nutmeg
- 2 drops of stevia
- 1 teaspoon cinnamon
- 3 tablespoon ghee

Directions

1. Slice apples and add the listed ingredients (alongside sliced apples) to your Slow Cooker

2. Place lid and cook on LOW for 4 hours

3. Open lid and serve apples with Ice Cream

4. Enjoy!

Nutrition Values (Per Serving)

- Calories: 339
- Fat: 12g
- Carbohydrates: 32g
- Protein: 27g

(Prepping time: 20 minutes\ Cooking time: 6 to 7 hour 30 minutes |For 4 servings)

Ingredients

- 2 cups caramelized onions and garlic
- 3 large carrots, peeled and chopped
- 8 cups roasted vegetable broth
- 5 tablespoon red bell pepper paste
- 1 bay leaf
- 1 teaspoon dried dill weed
- 1 cup coconut cream
- 2 tablespoons arrowroot

Directions

7. Add beets, onion, vegetable broth, carrots, pepper paste, bay leaf and dill weed
8. Cover and cook on LOW for 6-7 hours until the beets and carrots are tender
9. Remove lid and discard bay leaf
10. Use an immersion blender to puree the soup
11. Mix a bit of soup liquid with arrowroot and coconut cream and stir the mixture into soup
12. Cover and cook on LOW for 15-20 minutes until soup thickens

Nutrition Values (Per Serving)

- Calories: 239
- Fat: 8g
- Carbohydrates: 31g
- Protein: 10g

Chapter 10: Snacks And Appetizers Recipes

Lovely Potato Hash

(Prepping time: 10 minutes\ Cooking time: 4 hours |For 2 servings)

Ingredients

- 1 medium orange pepper, sliced and diced, deseeded
- 1 medium yellow pepper, sliced and diced, deseeded
- 10 and ½ ounces sweet potato
- 1 tablespoon coconut oil
- 1 teaspoon garlic puree
- 1 teaspoon thyme
- 1 teaspoon mustard powder
- Salt and pepper as needed

Directions

1. Dice the vegetables and potatoes and transfer to your Slow Cooker
2. Add coconut oil and seasoning
3. Mix
4. Cover with lid and cook on LOW for 4 hours
5. Serve and enjoy!

Nutrition Values (Per Serving)

- Calories: 270
- Fat: 10g
- Carbohydrates: 39g
- Protein: 5g

(Prepping time: 20 minutes\ Cooking time: 4 hours |For 4 servings)

Ingredients

- 24 ounce cremini mushrooms
- 4 garlic cloves, minced
- ½ teaspoon dried basil
- ½ teaspoon dried oregano
- 2 tablespoon parsley, minced
- 1 bay leaf
- 1 cup vegetable stock
- ¼ cup coconut milk
- 2 tablespoon ghee
- Sea salt as needed
- Freshly ground black pepper

Directions

1. Add the mushrooms, herbs and garlic to your slow cooker
2. Pour vegetable stock to the cooker and season
3. Cover and cook on LOW for 4 hours
4. Add coconut milk, stir and cook for a while until it is warm
5. Discard the bay leaf and season again
6. Serve!

Nutrition Values (Per Serving)

- Calories: 190
- Fat: 1g
- Carbohydrates: 40g
- Protein: 8g

(Prepping time: 5 minutes\ Cooking time: 6 hours |For 4 servings)

Ingredients

- 1 large cauliflower head
- 6 garlic cloves, peeled
- 4 tablespoon mixed herbs, minced
- 1 cup vegetable broth
- 4-6 cups water
- 3 tablespoons ghee
- Salt as needed

Directions

1. Peel up the leaves from your cauliflower and cut them up into medium florets
2. Add them to your cooker and top them up with garlic cloves, veggie broth and just enough water to cover the cauliflower
3. Cook on LOW for 6 hours and then on HIGH for 3 hours
4. Drain the water and broth and add the cauliflower back to the cooker
5. Add butter and use immersion blender to mash them
6. Season with some salt and pepper
7. Add herbs for added flavor
8. Serve and enjoy!

Nutrition Values (Per Serving)

- Calories: 25
- Fat: 5g
- Carbohydrates: 0g
- Protein: 2g

(Prepping time: 10 minutes\ Cooking time: 3 hours |For 6 servings)

Ingredients

- 3 cups raw pecans
- ¼ cup date paste
- 2 teaspoons vanilla bean extract
- 1 teaspoon sea salt
- 1 tablespoon coconut oil

Directions

1. Add all of the listed ingredients to your pot
2. Cook on LOW for about 3 hours, making sure to stir it from time to time
3. One done, allow it to cool and serve!

Nutrition Values (Per Serving)

- Calories : 337
- Fat : 31g
- Carbohydrates : 16g
- Protein::4g

(Prepping time: 10 minutes\ Cooking time: 2 hours |For 6 servings)

Ingredients

- 6 cups cashews
- 3 tablespoons coconut oil
- 1 tablespoon stevia
- Pinch of salt
- 2 tablespoon dried thyme
- 3 tablespoons dried rosemary leaves
- ¾ teaspoon paprika
- ½ teaspoon onion powder
- ½ teaspoon garlic powder

Directions

1. Heat your Slow Cooker by setting it to HIGH settings (for 15 minutes)
2. Add cashews and drizzle coconut oil over the cashews
3. Take a small bowl and add the spices, mix them well
4. Add the spices over the cashews and toss to coat them
5. Cover with lid and cook on LOW for 2 hours, making sure to keep stirring it after every hour
6. Remove the lid and cook for 30 minutes more
7. Serve and enjoy!

Nutrition Values (Per Serving)

- Calories : 352
- Fat : 21g
- Carbohydrates : 25g
- Protein : 14g

(Prepping time: 10 minutes\ Cooking time: 6 hours |For 8 servings)

Ingredients

- 1 bottle of (12 ounce) hot pepper sauce
- ½ cup melted ghee
- 1 tablespoons dried oregano
- 2 teaspoons garlic powder
- 1 teaspoon onion powder
- 5 pounds chicken wing sections

Directions

1. Take a large bowl and mix hot sauce, ghee, garlic powder, oregano, onion powder and mix
2. Add chicken wings and toss them to coat well
3. Pour mix into Slow Cooker insert
4. Cover and cook on LOW for 6 hours
5. Serve and enjoy!

Nutrition Values (Per Serving)

- Calories: 529
- Fat: 4g
- Carbohydrates: 1g
- Protein: 31g

(Prepping time: 15 minutes\ Cooking time: 10 hours |For 4 servings)

Ingredients

- 1-2 tablespoons Dijon mustard
- 1 tablespoon olive oil
- 2 tablespoon apple cider vinegar
- Salt and pepper as needed
- 1 teaspoon dried rosemary
- 4 medium potato, peeled and cubed
- 11 medium onions, chopped

Directions

1. Take a medium sized bowl and add mustard, apple cider and oil
2. Mix them well and season the mixture with salt and pepper
3. Add potatoes and onion and give it a nice stir
4. Grease your slow cooker with cooking spray and transfer the prepared mixture to your Slow Cooker
5. Cover and cook on LOW for 10 hours
6. Once the potatoes are tender, enjoy!

Nutrition Values (Per Serving)

- Calories: 196
- Fat: 4g
- Carbohydrates: 37g
- Protein: 4g

CHAPTER 11: STOCKS AND SAUCES

ROASTED VEGETABLE BROTH

(Prepping time: 20 minutes\ Cooking time: 6-8 hours |For 12 servings)

Ingredients

- 2 onions, peeled and chopped
- 1 leek, chopped
- 3 carrots, cut into 2 inch pieces
- 2 celery stalks, cut into 2 inch pieces
- 4 garlic cloves, smashed
- 1 tablespoon olive oil
- 1 tablespoon fresh lemon juice
- 1 bay leaf
- ½ teaspoon salt
- 10 cups water

Directions

1. Take a large roasting pan and add onions, leek, celery, carrots
2. Drizzle olive oil and toss
3. Roast for 20 minutes at 375 degree Fahrenheit in your oven until the veggies are light brown
4. Add veggies and remaining ingredients to your Slow Cooker
5. Close lid and cook on LOW for 6-8 hours
6. Remove lid and use a tong to remove any solids, discard the solids
7. Strain broth through cheesecloth into a large bowl
8. Divide the broth into 1 cup portions and use as needed

Nutrition Values (Per Serving)

- Calories : 30
- Fat : 1g
- Carbohydrates : 5g
- Protein:: 1g

(Prepping time: 10 minutes \ Cooking time: 7-10 hours |For 14 servings)

Ingredients

- 6 bone-in, skinless chicken thighs
- 2 celery stalks, cut into 2 inch pieces
- 2 large carrots, cut into 2 inch chunks
- 1 onion, cut into 6 wedges
- 12 cups water
- 1 teaspoon peppercorns
- ½ teaspoon salt
- 1 bay leaf

Directions

1. Add the listed ingredients to your Slow Cooker
2. Stir and close lid
3. Cook on LOW for 7-10 hours
4. Remove lid and discard the solids
5. Strain the stock through cheesecloth into a large bowl
6. Divide the stock into 2 cup portions and use as needed!

Nutrition Values (Per Serving)

- Calories : 40
- Fat : 2g
- Carbohydrates : 1g
- Protein: 4g

(Prepping time: 15 minutes\ Cooking time: 4-6 hours |For 14 servings)

Ingredients

- 2 pounds shrimp shells, fish bones, crab shells
- ½ cup leek, chopped
- 11 cups water
- 1 tablespoon freshly squeezed lemon juice
- 1 onion, cut into wedges
- 5 garlic cloves, peeled and smashed
- ½ teaspoon white peppercorns
- ½ teaspoon salt
- 2 cups red bell pepper, deseeded and sliced
- ½ teaspoon dried thyme leaves

Directions

1. Add the listed ingredients to your Slow Cooker
2. Stir
3. Cover with lid and cook on LOW for 4-6 hours
4. Remove lid
5. Discard any solids from the stock and strain stock through cheesecloth into a l large bowl
6. Divide the stock in 1 cup portions and use as needed

Nutrition Values (Per Serving)

- Calories : 63
- Fat : 2g
- Carbohydrates : 2g
- Protein:: 8g

CONCLUSION

I can't express how honored I am to think that you found my book interesting and informative enough to read it all through to the end.

I thank you again for purchasing this book and I hope that you had as much fun reading it as I had writing it.

I bid you farewell and encourage you to move forward with your amazing Lectin-Free Slow Cooker journey!